A Woman of Faith With a Legacy of Love

**A collection of writings, poems, and songs of
Delores Ann Williams (Wilburn)**

Dedicated by your children

Our mother wore many hats in her lifetime. She was a daughter, wife, mother, writer, giver, usher, and friend, and student just to name a few.

Our mom's soft-spoken words and loud roaring laughter kept me hanging off her every bit. I didn't realize how much of a talent our mom had for writing and biblical knowledge until after she passed on to be with her creator. What for sure I saw her model my whole life was her love for her family, all people, God, and the scriptures. In my forty plus years of living, I didn't hear a single curse word come from her lips. I can't even say the same for me. Actually, I can't recall any negative words or conversation because even if she disagreed with a person, she still did so with so much grace. I'm certainly not trying to paint her as perfect, no human born is. Mom had a way of expressing her frustrations in a way that didn't insult the person or topic she was frustrated about.

Our mom's legacy of Faith is left with me. She lived a Psalm chapter 23 kind of life. Any problem I told her about she responded by telling me to pray. Mom didn't want for much, the still waters were always beside her, and she stayed on a path of righteousness. I saw her Faith in God alive and thriving up until her depart. We were with her in that shadow of death. The passage speaks to me because she was walking through the valley but it felt like I was in the shadow. She thanked God, read her Bible, and prayed more times then I'd seen her not. She had so many testimonies I knew nothing about until recently. That kind of Faith that she displayed challenges me to have even bigger Faith in my everyday life. To see her continue to trust God, and not relent one moment is the legacy of Faith she left behind.

Our mom's legacy of love is seen in all her children, grandchildren, and many other relatives and friends. The way mom loved God and people is something that I can only hope to measure close to one day. She loved to give,

1

serve, and help people in any capacity she could. It was in form of transporting people to and fro, giving food, or household items, serving at her church, or even on her job or within the community. She was always going above and beyond even when I told her she was extending herself too much. Her Love was just that big.

You will see her Faith in God, Love of family, friends, and service, as well as her talents, and abilities throughout these pages. Although I wish I knew about them so much sooner. It will be impossible to not see the hand of God throughout her life. May this collection bless, delight, and encourage you. Mom was not one to boast so I hope she doesn't mind that I'm sharing these works from the woman that we called, "Mother" with you. May these words inspire you to live a higher calling, may her examples push you to love deeper, may her testimonies help you develop a stronger faith, and motivate you to leave a legacy of your own.

3

Part 1

Her Faith in Action

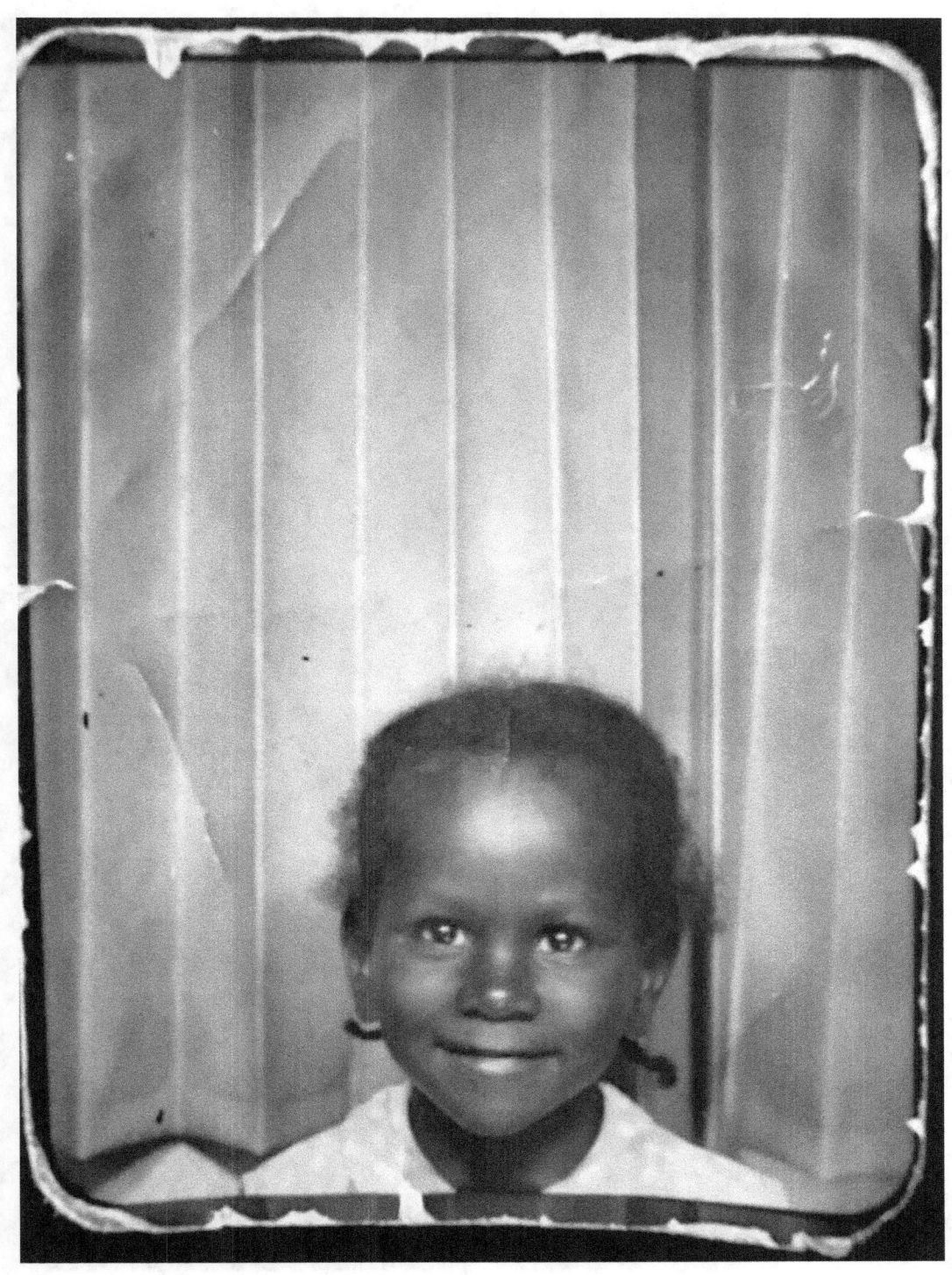

My Apartment Testimony

Around the beginning of Dec. 1975 I was put out of the house. (During this period I was tarrying for the Holy Ghost) Being that I'd never looked for a place to stay before because I'd never lived alone, I didn't know where to even start looking for an apartment. I just got my Soc. Sec. check and started walking. I decided to walk on by a friends house. I headed for the bus stop. I was just going to hop on a bus going towards downtown I still didn't have any idea where I was going to go. The bus had gotten downtown and as I was looking around my eyes caught the letters YMCA. I tentively got off the bus. The Lord eventually led me to the YWCA. I found that in order to get a room there one had to call 2 wks. ahead. They didn't have any rooms for sure. I was told to come back later. (next day) When I came back I found that the Lord had cleared a room for me. He let a lady leave early. My hostess said, as she was taking me to my room she didn't think the room had even been cleaned-up yet. But, when we got there we found a clean room with clean linen and towels, and soap. God not only let the lady leave but he let them give me a clean room. After living there a number of wks. and staying in different rooms a Sister at church let me move in with her. She knew where I could get an

9

apartment for $85.00 a month.
At the YWCA I found myself
spending about $80.00 a month. I
had to pay for a room, buy food on
everyday, because, I had no pots & pans
no silverware, a threat of getting any
groceries stollen cause everyone on the
floor shared the kitchen. (I got a
chance to witness to a girl who
had been in a coma for a year.)
I moved out. While staying with the
sister I talked with the landlord.
And do you know he held an apart
ment for me on a $10.00 deposit. That
was just the Lord. Well I had
my apartment but not one stick of
furniture, except a bedroom suit at
my mother's house over 30 miles away.
But, you know the Lord blessed and

10

filled my apartment with furniture.

{ My main point in this testimony is how the Lord let the landlord hold this apartment for me (about 2 to 2½ wks) on a $10.00 deposit }

Testimony
God Will Provide

Living in my apartment I ran into financial difficulty. I was out of school for a semester my Soc. Sec. was cut off. I had no income. Prior to this I applied for financial aide at school. Well it came during this hardship but I was told I couldn't cash it. It was over 300 dollars. I started to tear it up, but, decided to put it away in an old purse. Things got worse. I eventually ran completely out of food. No food no where in the house. All I had in the house on the line was water some baking soda with in the refrig. I was unable to pay rent or DPL. This went on for about 2 to 2½ months. The landlord

12

tried to bear with me cause I was a good Tennant. But finally he gave me 2 wks or I would have to leave. During this time I got a job, worked for 2 wks. and was fired. I only made $21.00 total. Finally I decided to get that check from the purse and go to the school and check into whether I can cash it or not. I decided to try once more. I went to the financial aide office and asked one of the main secretaries. She said yes. To double check I wanted to get permission from the President. Well it turned out that the Vice-President, I was told, oked it. Isn't God good. I was able to catch-up some and later I was back in shape again. During this whole crisis I never went a day hungry or never put out of doors. God will provide.

13

Car Testimony

no. 1

727 Ferguson

It was offering time at church. We were asked to give a special blessing offering. We were suposed to put in all our change. I didn't have any in my purse so I went to my coat and found 2¢. I put it in the offering. God blessed us with a Rebel for under $200.00 plus we were able to use the car while we paid on it.

no. 2

After using the Rebel for a while we moved to another location 995 Scottwood and used it another while before it gave up. After sitting a while it was towed away. We didn't have money for another car. We were living on the outskirts of Dayton, between Dayton and Madison twp. My husband worked at Frigidaire in Moraine City until he was layed off and it became a truck factory. When going to work he would get up and go out and thumb his way to work and back home. Sometimes he got riders. There were times he either got out because of what they were doing in their cars or they stopped picking him up. This went on for quite some time, then the Lord laid it on someone's heart to give us a 4 door Mazda station wagon free of charge. They even got it checked out for us and tuned up.

14

Car Testimony

No. 3

When we left 988 Scottswood we didn't have a car. Sometimes my husband drove the church van (he was the driver at that time for it) but that's not like your own transp. The Lord blessed us to be on the bus line. We couldn't always get a ride wherever we needed to go. Sometimes I had to carry 3 or 4 grocery bags on the bus; trying to get enough to last a while. Sometimes was worse than others when it was cold. Then when we couldn't get a ride to church; we'd pack up our 3 kids, diaper bag, guitar, briefcase, all our stuff and get on the bus rain or shine and even in the cold most times. I had one child in the christian school. Sometimes we could not get a ride. *Sometimes we would miss the bus and have to run a few streets over to catch it when it turned around.* I'd have to get up early enough to get her to school on the bus cause she was to small to go by herself. Then again to get her back home. (Sad to say, friends saw us and left us in the cold and rain.) Then when we moved again that made matters worse. We were futher away and it took 2 buses one way. There were times when I couldn't make my connections in time to get her to or from school on time. Or even got on the wrong bus cause there we a with the same no. but one stopped abt 2½ miles short of where sch. was. I really had to cry sometimes; but I was determined my child was going to the christian school. Finally, one of the saints gave us a car (his work car) for a very small sum. The car was abt. 18 yrs. old (still running good) but it looked like gold to me.

No. 4

During the time period when Bishop was asking for $50.00 to $100.00 in the offering I sat there wanting to do something. I wanted to put in a big offering like that. I'm just a housewife with no job. Prior to that I had the philosophy that even a wife should have something in the bank to cushion her if for some reason her husband was no longer there. So I scratched and scraped over a period of months. Then the Lord laid it on my heart to give $25.00 in Sun. offer. That was all I had. Prior to that I had decided that I wouldn't touch this money for any reason. I over-rode that idea and gave a few days later I told my

15

Glasses

When I first came to Christ Temple I wore glasses.

I was told by doctors that I had to wear them at all times.

I was a babe in the Lord, so one day I took my glasses off and laid them on the seat and I was shouting in the spirit. Well, when I came down I noticed that someone had sat on my glasses. They were broken. Well after that the Lord began to tell me through different saints that he could heal my eyes. I never got my glasses fixed. The Lord blessed me to get my drivers liscence and to function perfectly without them

thought came to me in Mass Choir Rehearsal 8/24/77 1st Week Evangelist preached Pertaing to it 8/29

So I drew it in Rehearsal today

They Cruisefied My Lord

thorns

hysop to drink

Blood
&
Water

Blood Sweat

He Never Said A Mumbling Word

17

Testimony

Had a Baby

I got married on April 2, 1977. The Lord blessed us to concieve not long afterwards. I had a miscarriage in my early months. This went on a number of times. Then I concieved again. My doctor told me I had to ly down for 4 straight hours a day. Well I did lay down a while for a few days. Then I told myself I was going to trust the Lord. So I forgot what the doctor said. We had just moved into Christ Temple on Denlinger. The church has a lot of stairs. But, I went to church. I climbed those stairs, I fasted when the church did, I testified and I praised God. The Lord Blessed and we gave

18

birth to a healthy 10 lbs 10 1/4 oz. baby girl.

Note: Before I became pregnant there was another Sis. Williams in our church who was in the hospital and had just had a baby. She was having a problem so she called Eld. Lofton in the middle of the night. While he was talking to her on the phone, he thought that she was me. So he prayed for me. I became pregnant abt. a month later.

Note:

(Even though I was conceiving and miscarrying the doctor or nurse told me that usually with the particular problem I had a woman would not concieve.)

Healing of Our Baby

After our first child was born. (the one doctors thought I would lose). They told us that she had advanced bonage, which meant she was growing too fast. She was about 6 months. They wanted to run all kinds of test on her. We didn't let them. So they started drawing up paper to take her away from us. There were case workers coming to our house anytime they got ready. This went on for a while. We were advised by our pastor and his wife to let them run test. We did. They basically tortured our child. They sent her through all these test. They said such things as...

If it is this then she'll only have to have a shot abt. every three months. They just kept looking. Finally they told us bring her back in 3 months. Well we didn't. The doctors that examined her we never heard from them again, nor the case workers.

Then one morning the clinic where we took our child for health care called us because we had missed a clinic apt. (They were the ones who started all the trouble) They told us we had missed an apt. and they said, "By the way" the doctors could not find anything wrong with your baby. So the doctors didn't tell us anything, We just heard it through the grapevine!

21

4, 1978

(Poem No. 1) Just a little note to say
I are thinking about you today
And I would like you to know
I remember you when I pray.

(Poem No. 2) Just a little note to say
I thought about you today
I'll remember you when I pray.

My Testimony

You can't tell it   (CANN'T)
Like I do   (or tell it)
What the Lord has done

So many things
He's done for me
When no one could
He set my soul free

Gave me the courage
To do His will
In serving Him wholely
My life is fullfilled

22

HOPE OF SALVATION

Saved by the Gospel,
Saved by Grace,
Don't you know,
I've got to run this race.

Got to hear my name,
Called out on high,
God's going to bless me,
By and by.

Jesus is coming,
Soon again,
No need of running,
Ducking your chin.

Where you're going to run,
No place to hide,
Just get your life in order,
And with Him you'll abide.

My hope is in that city,
Up yonder on high,
And when my saviour calls,
I'll meet Him in the sky.

Going to live with him forever,
In His eternal bliss,
And what the world has had to offer,
Will not at all be missed.

Author: Delores Williams

VICTORY IN JESUS

Bold as a lion,
Bold as a bear,
Thanks be to Jesus,
For getting us out of a snare.

The snare of wickedness, sin and pride,
The state of which made Adam to hide,
God needed to redeem his creation,
So he made himself a body and dwelt inside.

He came down from above,
With men to dwell,
To save men's souls,
And keep them out of hell.

He cast out demons,
Healed the blind,
Gave speech to the speechless,
And healed people's minds.

He healed the deaf,
And raised the dead,
Gave sense to the lunatick,
And kept the widow fed.

He loved little children,
With them he did talk,
He even taught great multitudes,
And made the lame to walk.

He healed the leper,
And calmed the sea,
Walked on water,
Examples for you and me.

Victory in Jesus,
For you and me,
Salvation in his name,
Throughout eternity.

Author: Delores Williams

S E L F

There's no room for self,
In the life of a saint,
Cause next thing you know,
It'll make you an ain't.

It'll cause you to lie,
And to steal and fight,
And before you notice,
Heaven's out of your sight.

It'll cause emulation,
Sedition and strife,
Evil concupiscence,
You know that's not right.

Adultery, witchcraft, varience,
You know,
That's the wrong way to do it,
And the wrong way to go.

So let's turn around,
And see our way clear,
With love, joy, and peace,
Which makes this way so dear,
And Heaven so near.

Author: Delores Williams

THE ROCKS CRY OUT

Don't sing,
Don't pray,
Or even talk about,
The things that God has done for you,
Or how he brought you out.

He stopped you from drinking,
From staggering around,
He even got you up,
Off that filthy ground.

He took the smoke,
Whatever kind it may be,
He really cares,
But that you don't see.

He stopped you from gambling,
Losing all you've got,
Try so hard,
To make a lot.

He stopped you from stealing,
Trying to see what you can get,
Without paying for it.

He stopped the hooker,
From turing her tricks,
Took her off the street corner,
Now she can resist.

The things you did,
The things you do,
You think you're something,
Don't you?

He don't need you,
Who are you anyway?
Just look at what he's done for you,
And you turn your face away.

You don't have to praise him,
The rocks will cry out,
And he'll be praised anyway.

Author: Delores Williams

26

THE NEW JERUSALEM

God made a city,
Pure, clean, and bright,
For those who would serve him,
And walk in his light.

He gave us a choice,
And gave us a space,
Hoping we'd choose to,
In peace see his face.

He gave us a reason,
To serve him in life,
So we wouldn't spend eternity,
In pain, shame and fright.

Oh! New Jerusalem,
Your streets paved with gold,
The devil tried to get me,
But I was not sold.

You see, I love my Jesus,
For all that he has done,
I would never desert him,
For nothing under the sun.

Author: Delores Williams

I SEE A VISION

The body of Christ,
None other is like,
One of Great Stamina,
Power and might.

None can compare,
Or even share,
The Glory, the majesty,
He's everywhere.

The Alpha and Omega,
The beginning and end,
He's obnificent,
He saves men from sin.

He gives life a reason,
Anytime, any season.

Author: Delores Williams

WAY TO GO

The river of Zion,
Oh! What a sight,
That's why we should serve him,
With all our might,
Both day and night.

Serve him now,
Don't clown around,
It'll all be over,
When they put you in the ground.

Remember now thy creator,
In the days of thy youth,
Yes, that's in the book,
Just take a look.

Ecclesiastes 12:1,
That's where it's at,
Now how about that!

Determine your destiny,
While there's still time,
Know God's Word,
That'll keep you in line.

                    Author: Delores Williams

29

L O V E

The love,
That Jesus shows,
Will never grow old.

He keeps it alive,
Through you and me,
Even to the end,
Throughout eternity.

He gave us the choice,
Who we should serve,
Him or men,
Who shall it be.

Earthly riches,
And fame,
What is the gain,
When all that really counts,
Is in his name.

Author: Delores Williams

CALVARY

At the cross of calvary,
My Saviour died for me,
Twas at this very special place,
He set my captive soul free.

It took a very special person,
One who did no sin,
To bear the cross in agony,
To die and live again.

He made an heavenly city,
For us to live within,
He made the way at calvary,
For us to enter in.

And when the time had come,
He left this earthly reign,
And though he ascended up from the earth,
He's coming back again.

Author: Delores Williams

T I M E

What time is it,
What time it's not,
I think we'd better,
Give this some thought.

What's wrong with time,
Or is it me,
I just can't see,
What it may be.

Am I too slow?
Is it too fast?
Or does it go by,
With a flash?

There's too few hours,
In a day,
That's why we ought,
To watch and pray.

It is high time,
To awake out of sleep,
Do what you should,
Join force with the meek.

Give praise to God,
Anytime, any season.
Praise Him for what?
Time is the reason!

Time to be saved,
Is what he's gave,
And with his grace,
We'll do it by faith.

Author: Delores Williams

THE WILDERNESS PERIOD

There comes a time,
In the child of God's life,
Where are you Jesus?
Please hear my cry!

I've prayed and prayed,
Seems you don't hear,
What's the matter?
Have you disappeared?

I've examined myself,
I Am Still Strong!!
My life is clean,
So what's wrong?

Am I being tested,
To see what I'll do?
If that's the case,
I've made up my mind,
And I'm walking with you.

Whatever comes my way,
I've decided to stay,
Cause serving you Jesus,
Is the only way.

Author: Delores Williams

God's Sacraficial Love

I don't know why
My savior died
To be a sacrifice
For a wretch like I

Why make the way
For me to live again
When all I was doing
Is waldling in sin

Having a good time
Doing all I could
That ol' enemy
He made it look good

Yet, God saw my need
And knew I'd take heed
He sent me a witness
And I took the seed

I kept it at heart
Never let it part
Then time and chance happened to me
And I made a start

Started living for Jesus
Happy as can be
That he saw fit
To save a wretch like me.

34

Tell It
Go tell it

Living a Holy and a Sanctified life
Serving my Jesus with all my might
Trying to do the best that I can
Cause with him I want to live again)

Telling the people of God's Word
Some, you know, have not heard
They do not know what God can do
Because they haven't heard it, from me and you

Tell them he saves men from their sins
Tell them that they can live again
Tell them there's no secret what God can do
Cause, what he's done for others he'll do the same
for you

Tell Me Why

I don't know why
My mama had to die
I don't know why
But you do

I don't know why
She had to suffer so
I don't know why Lord
But you do

I don't know why
That's my thought
I don't know why
But you do

I don't know why
And that hurts so
I don't know why
But you do

Lord I don't know why
A love that's lost
I don't know why
But you do

Lord, I don't know why
But you do
And I leave it with you

The things people say
The things they do
God gave me the strength
To stand up to you

I won't give up
Nor either back down
God gave me the Holyghost
It won't let me down

37

By The River

The beauty of the Stream
The smell of fresh rain
The air so clean
The flowers bloom Blown again
The birds they do sing
Of Heavenly things
The animals do talk
As they take a walk

The Birds and the Bees
The kissing of the Trees
As the wind blows through the leaves
It creates a breeze

The smell of fresh rain
Comming Coming down from above
Sent from the father
In pure, sweet, love

The flowers they bloom
For us to see
Food grows to
For your and me

Mortgage Retirement

The Little Church Who Did

Together we stand
Devided we fall
We tried it and
We gave it our all

We knew it would work
We didn't give up
We wouldn't be told
It was too much

They said we couldn't (do it)
But we did
Just look around
Our proof is not hid

We did it mightely
As unto the Lord
And he did bless
With great reward.

① Waking up this morning
Jesus was on my mind
He started me out on the right foot
He started me right on time

② Stirring towards my journey
He said whey Don't you listen to me
For there is something I want you to do
If you'll just come on
   And walk beside me

③ You have no reason for fearing   · FEARING
For I'll allways be near
If you just stay, stay on the right track
And don't let Satan I don't let him
                        turn you
                              back

④ Just keep your heart in the right place
And your ~~mind~~ mind stayed on Jesus
For He, He is your redeemer
Bless His precious name

⑤ the Lord is my shepperd (SHEPPARD)
And I shall not want
He supplies my every need,
He is my, He is my all indeed

④ So when your soul gets hungry
Just call, call out His name
For He, He will be there
If you just trust in my God's name

Chorus for the chorus repeat verses
              1-4 with a faster
                              tempo

40

God gave me this Song. He started it before I was saved or even went to Christ Temple. He finished it after I got saved. Also I have no name for it. I got the

Why Don't You Listen

→ title in 1979
say it in 1978

(1)
Waking up this morning
Jesus was on my mind
He started me out on the right foot
He started me right on time

(2)
Striving towards my journey
He said "Why don't you listen to me?"
There is something, I want you to do
If you just come on and walk beside me

(3)
You have no reason for fearing
For I'll always be near
If you just stay, stay on the right track
And don't let Satan, don't let him turn you back

(4)
Just keep your heart in the right place
And your mind stayed on Jesus
For he, He is your Redeemer
Bless his precious name

(5)   1976 below
The Lord is my shepherd And I shall not want
And I shall not want
He supplies my every need
He is my, He is my all indeed

(6)
So when your soul gets hungry
Just call, Call out his name
For he, He will be there
If you just trust in my God's name

The Lord gave me before I was Saved

41

Part 2

Delores the Student

Our mother had many beliefs, dispositions, and temperaments to her credit. I hadn't realized how fervent she was in her beliefs until discovering many recorded lessons in her own penmanship. As far as I can remember from what she told us over the years, she wasn't very religious as a child. She did attend church though. But apparently in her late teens and early twenties she was quite curious about faith, religion, and all the topics that was taught concerning it.

It was after I began to read over the notes she'd kept for many years, that I found she had a deep passion for learning and growing in her Christian faith. A passion that kept her researching the Bible, studying it, and testing her knowledge from what she had learned. As a matter of fact, the subject must've been so important to her that she continued to soak up all she could, even after my sister and I were born. Although, I can't possibly understand how she found the time to study, prepare for tests, or many of the things that she did during new motherhood. But the discipline was certainly passed down to her children.

In this next section, you will get to know Delores as the student. Just so you know, the following will only be a fraction of the documents she deemed as important enough to be saved for all these years. Though I feel you will get the jest of her work. You'll find that she didn't make perfect grades. However, it will be hard not to be aware of the thought and preparation she put into every single page.

Our mother implemented many of her talents throughout her life. We were blessed enough to be on the direct receiving end of many of them. These next pages you will turn, occurred before all of her children were born. Approximately between 1975 - 1981. But how fortunate we are to have them still and share them for all to see. It was plain for me to understand how dedicated she was to being a good steward and student. It was also evident in any area of her life that she committed to. I would be remised to not mention her teachers and other ministerial figures who put just as much dedication and effort into helping her learn and succeed. Without any further a due, Delores the Student.

43

Sensori-motor

Mrs. Leedy

Delores Wilburn

The Story of Sandy

by Susan Stanhope Wexler

A Signet Book from New American Library

+7

This is the story of a little boy named Sandy. In this paper I intend to tell you of how he was so denied love that he showed no emotins physicallyand hardly showed any signs of life.

Sandy was born to a couple named Mary and Tommy. Mary, when she was a child, was one of two twins. She had a twin brother. In her mind she could remember, while brushing her hair in the bedroom dressor mirror, that her parents did not want a klittle girl,but a little boy. She was completely denied all the love and affection that was given unto her twin brother. Tommy, when he was a child, was adopted by two foster parents named Joe and Sukey. They lived in Chicago. They showed To Tommy very much love an d affection that is normally given to a child.

When Tommy and Mary became engaged he took her to Chicago to his parents home. After staying there a while, Mary began telling Sukey agout her child live. She told Sukey about her twin brother. She also told her about other storys that were supposed to have happened. She told many storys and her personality seemed to change with each one. She had very bad feelings about her early life.

While carrying Sandy, Mary had problems. The aurthor did not mention what these problems were. Tommy was very worried all during her pregnancy. Finally, a redheaded, freckle-faced and healthy child was born /. His name was Sandy.

In the beginning Mary seemed to love and cherish her child just like any other mother who has just had her first child. As time went on, Mary began to remember of how she was treated because of her little twin brother who just happed to be a boy. She began denying to Sandy the love and affection that was so brutally denied to her by both her parents.

50

When Sandy was six years of age he was so unloved and unpetted thathe didn't even mumble of try to talk.Physically he just lay there and didn't even wiggle where ever he was put. He was so mistreated that he was afraid to waste any of his food when feeding himself. Atter a while, Mary tried to admit him to a retarded home for children. Tommy, being that he was a foster child, could not completely agree to this so one stromy and snowy night he called Sukey to ask if he could catch the one o'clock train to bring Sandy to her. At six o'clock the next morning they arrived. Sukey had everything ready for a three year old child. While telling them everything, Tommy broke down and cried for the first time in years. Sukey t ok Sandy to bed. The next day she began giving Sandy the love and affection that was denied to him by his mother. For the first time he began to make that silly laughing noise that a six month old baby makes. HE even began to sit up when he was placed to do so. Even when he was put to bed he began to rock himself to get a little comfort and love from himself. It was not until six months later that he began to cry in the night.

In this paper I tried tosay that when a child is denied love and affection it can have a great physical and psycological affect upon his life. By getting Sandy into different surroundings and under the influence of other parents that gave him lov and affection he later began to improve.

51

My Reactions

I think that the aurthor's main idea is that when Mary was a child she was denied all the love and affection that was given to her twin brother and so when she had a son she, in turn, denied to him all the love and affection that was earlier denied to her by both of her parents. Sandy was not a retarded child as every one seemed to think. The aurthor seemed to show you this in his step by step method of developement. What I mean by this is that he began from the beginning of Sandy's life instead of waiting until elsewhere. I except the book because it is really a true story.

There must be something that they did that you wouldn't do or something that you would do that they didn't.

How could you use what you read in the classroom?

Mrs. Adair
Soc. Problems   Soc 111 10
Delores Wilburx
Oct. 16, 1975

53

A alternative To Marriage

This ~~book~~ article is basically pertaining to couples who live together but are not married. A study was made of thirty one going together couples and eighteen living together couples. The study showed that the going together couples had a strong committment towards marriage. Also that they had other important feelings. The living together couples had less interest in other feelings. The living togerher women seemed to want security while the men seemed to want an alternative. In another test the "pill" was stated as an accepted way of life and also that it reduced the concern of unwanted pregnancies because of increased sexual activities.

In my opinion, if a couple really cares about each other they can wait on marriage liscensed rather than living together and acting accordingly. I feel that it is more to marriage than sexual freedoms. To me (in plain language) when a couple is living together a man just gets what ever he can free and if he doesn't really care for the woman he can just get up and walk out on her the next morning(or even the next five minutes)without anything to worry him. He doesn't have to worryabout the woman throwing a big fat case against him in a court of law. The woman can not get any type of support. If it was unwillfully proceded she may have a chance. Under the circumstances, she has no way of proving this or a very slim chance. If one looks for the opposite sex who has more of the same feelings rather than looking for one with a better sex abllity, marriage rates may be higher while divorce rates may be lower. Concerning the pill, I feel that no woman needs it for the simple reason if she is not doing anything wrong in the first place she has nothing to worry about such as unwanted pregnancy.

Bibliography

American Family

Vincent 1966   discussion of changing family func.

Winch 1970   Predic. of declin. marriage rates in

                                           the future

The research was partially supported bya an N I M H Research Grant, RO3MH17663-01

by an award from the U. of Col. Council on Research and Creative Work,

awarded to the two junior authors, and by an N I M H Predoctoral Research

Fellowship, 7FO1MH3253-02, to the first aut or. The research was conducted

during the period summer 1969 through summer 1970.

Small Is Beautiful

This book is based on things in history such as; The Nobel Prize.
It talks on to the reader to say that in 1969 the Nobel Prize was estab-
lished for economic science. This was suposed to put them on the same level
as psychaiatrists, biologists, and ect. It deals a little on Erik Lundberg
who observed that economic science had developed increasibly in the direction
of mathematical specification and statistical qualification of ecomomic contexts.

At first I could not understand why the author called this book "Small Is
Beautiful" whie he is talking on such broad subjects. For example, The Nobel
Prize, Economic Science, and The American Council of Economic Advisors. When
I read a little more I began to understand a little better. Basically, I
Ddidn't understand what I was reading about, but I will continue on to try
and do what I can. I know that the state of the economy means what the
condition is of the overall thing. I also know that Lundberg is the man that
is in charge of the whole project. I have heard a little more about Lundberg
and from what I hear he seemed to be alright. I feel that we do need a makeli
man like him over great situations like these because he seems to handle them
very well indeed. We need more of his background over the complete system.

<u>Bibliography</u>

Small Is Beautiful

    Economics

As If People Mattered

E. F. Schumacher

H arper and Row, Publishers

N ew York, Evanston, San Francisco, London

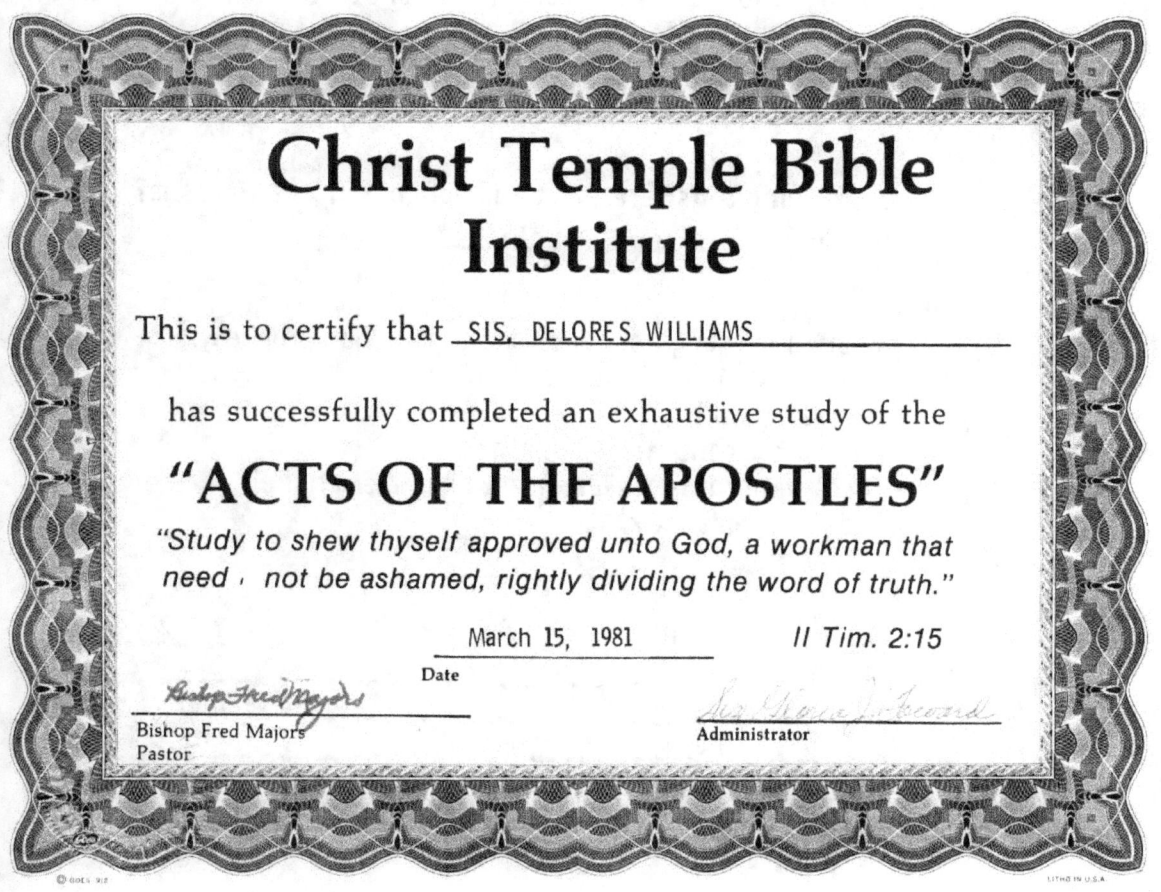

Christ Temple Bible Institute

This is to certify that _SIS. DELORES WILLIAMS_

has successfully completed an exhaustive study of the

"ACTS OF THE APOSTLES"

"Study to shew thyself approved unto God, a workman that need not be ashamed, rightly dividing the word of truth."

March 15, 1981   II Tim. 2:15

Date

Bishop Fred Majors   Administrator
Pastor

57

Sis. Delores Williams
Bro. Cargle's Class

70%

TEST #1   ACTS CHAPTERS 1 & 2

A. Multiple Choice
    1. Pentecost is associated with the number
        a) 5 (b) 50) c) 500 d) 5,000

    2. Acts were written to: a) Thomas (b) Theopilus) c) Peter d) Barnabas

B. Short Answer
    Acts 1:13
    3. Name the eleven original Apostles and the one chosen to be
        number 12. *Peter, Paul, Barnabus, Mark, Luke, John, Simon, Mathews, Bartholemew, James, Jude*
    4. Who was being considered, but was not chosen as an Apostle?
        (full name) *Mathias*

C. True or False
    5. *False* Your sons, daughters and young men shall prophesy.
    6. *False* The sun shall be turned to blood.
    7. *True* David foresaw the Lord always.
    8. *True* Alcedama means "field of blood"
    9. *True* There were three old testament characters named in
            Acts Chapters 1 & 2.

D. Memory Verse
    10. Then *Peter* said unto them, *Repent*, and be *baptised*
         everyone of you in the *name* of *Jesus Christ*
         for the *remission* of *sin*, and ye shall
         recieve the *gift* of the *Holy Ghost*.
         Acts *2:38*

58

Sons of the Profits - Bro Cargle's Class

90%   *Sis Delores. Williams*

TEST #2   ACTS CHAPTERS 3 & 4

A. I. Memory Verse   *Neither is there Salvation in any other*
      Quote Acts 4:12 *For there is none other name, under heaven,*
                      given among men whereby we must be
                      Saved.

B. Matching

   2. *B* Joses
   3. *D* Barnabas
   4. *A* Annas
   5. *E* Peter
   6. *C* Samuel

   a. High Priest
   b. Barnabas
   c. Prophet
   d. Son of Consolation
   e. Apostle

C. Short Answer

   7. There was a miracle done in Chapter three, name the three main
      characters *Peter*, *John*, and *the lame man (Impotent)*
      Name the specific location in Jerusalem of the miracle *Temple, at the gate beautiful*
      What was the miracle (be specific) *lame man was healed*? How old
      was the man who was healed *about fourty*.

D. True or False

   8. *False* The number of men who heard the word and believed was 3,000.
   9. *True* Caiaphas, John and Alexander were among the rulers, elders
            and scribes gathered to the trial of Peter and John.
   10. *True* Abraham, Isaac, Jacob, Samuel and David are the only old
             testament characters mentioned in Chapters 3 & 4.

59

Sis. Delores Williams
Bro. Cargle's Class

S

ACTS STUDY AID
Chapters 3 & 4

I Vocabulary Matching

H 1. Alms 3:2

A 2. Restitution 3:21

D 3. Covenant 3:25

J 4. Scribes 4:5

B 5. Salvation 4:12

I 6. Miracle 4:16

G 7. Manifest 4:16

O 8. Rage 4:25

L 9. Vain 4:25

N 10. Anointed 4:27

F 11. Heathen 4:25

E 12. Hearken 4:19

K 13. Impotent 4:9

M 14. Multitude 4:32

C 15. Perceived 4:13

A. restoration or re-establishment

B. deliverance from destruction

C. knew

D. contract between God and men

E. Listen carefully

F. gentile

G. made visible

H. free gift to the poor

I. An act that contradicts scientific law

J. teacher, writer

K. without strength

L. worthless

M. crowd

N. consecrated

O. uncontrolled anger

II Short Answer

16. What hour did Peter and John go to the temple? *Ninth* 3:1

17. What was this hour called? *hour of prayer* 3:1

18. Who asked alms? *lame man at the gate beautiful* 3:2

19. Peter said he had no *silver* and *gold* 3:6

20. Name the old testament characters mentioned in chapters 3 & 4.

~~*Isiah*~~ *Jacob* 3:13 *Isaac* 3:13

~~*David*~~ *Moses* 3:13 *Samuel* 3:22

Abraham 3:24

60

III True & False

_F_ 21. Peter and Barnabas were arrested for preaching the resurrection of Jesus. 4:2

_F_ 22. Caiaphas was the high priest. 4:6

_F_ 23. The council marvelled at the knowledge of Peter and John. 4:13

_T_ 24. The council commanded Peter and John not to speak or teach in the name of Jesus. 4:18

_T_ 25. Many sold their possessions and laid the prices at the Apostles' feet. 4:34

IV Multiple Choice

26. Joses was (a) a Levite b) an apostle c) a scribe d) an elder 4:36

27. With the high priest at the council was a) James b) Matthew (c) Thomas d) John 4:6

28. In Peter's second sermon he spoke of a) Solomon b) Isaac c) David (d) All of the above e) None of the above 3:13

29. The Temple gate was called a) Solomon's b) East c) Golden (d) Beautiful 3:2

30. Immediately after he was healed, the Lame man (a) leaped b) walked c) praised God d) cried 3:8

V. Research

How does Psalms 2:1 relate to this lesson on Acts?

The heathen rage — the scribes and pharesies upset about Peter & John preaching

Define the Sanhedrin.

Name generally given by writers on Jewish antiquities and history to the highest Jewish assembly for government in the time of our Lord.

Vocabulary Word Search

Find and circle the word meaning the same as the words listed below

restitution Restoration or re-establishment ✓   *salvation* Deliverance form destruction ✓

perceive Knew ✓   *covenant* Contract between God and men ∠

hearken Listen carefully ✓   *Heathen* Gentile ✓

manifest Made visible ✓   *alms* Free gift to the poor ✓

miracle An act that contradicts scientific law   *scribes* Teacher; writer

impotent Without strength ✓   *vain* Worthless ✓

multitude Crowd   *annointed* Consecrated ✓

rage Uncontrolled anger ✓

```
H  K  V  O  L  N  M  G  A  C  E
M  T  N  A  N  E  V  O  C  C  O
U  S  E  N  T  K  H  E  A  T  E
L  I  H  O  N  R  D  U  E  L  N
D  P  T  I  E  A  I  M  C  O  S
E  O  A  N  T  E  R  A  I  A  R
V  T  E  T  O  H  R  T  L  S  T
I  E  H  E  P  I  U  V  M  C  S
E  V  G  D  M  T  A  R  A  R  E
C  A  R  T  I  T  S  A  N  I  F
R  I  M  T  I  L  M  A  I  B  I
E  N  S  O  V  A  L  E  R  E  N
P  E  N  M  I  R  A  C  T  S  A
R  T  E  D  U  T  I  T  L  U  M
```

62

Locate the following characters, then with the remaining 30 letters name the most important character of all and his gift to us. (You must rearrange the letters)

S	B	S	U	I	T	N	O	P	A
D	A	V	I	D	J	A	Z	R	N
O	T	H	E	R	O	D	Y	E	N
F	S	I	P	R	E	A	E	D	A
N	A	B	R	A	H	A	M	N	S
S	E	S	O	M	I	S	A	A	C
R	B	H	R	A	S	A	L	X	G
E	O	C	R	U	E	A	C	E	&
T	C	B	S	U	S	T	I	L	O
E	A	E	S	S	O	H	T	A	O
P	J	O	H	N	J	H	H	S	C

Jesus
Abraham
Isaac
Jacob
Moses
Peter
John
David
Annas
Caiaphas
Alexander
Joses
Herod
Pontius

Jesus Christ of Nazareth

ANSWER: _Jesus Christ gave us the gift of the_
& Holy ghost so that we could live right
Holy Ghost (without sin) and be saved.

Memorize for Tuesday
Acts 3:6
3:16
4:12

63

Sis. Delores Williams
Bro. Cargle's class
90%

TEST #5 ACTS CHAPTERS 9 & 10

A. MATCHING

1. ___*B*___ Saul   *A.* A town
2. ___*E*___ Ananias   *B.* Blind
3. ___*D*___ Staight   *C.* Dorcas
4. ___*A*___ Lydda   *D.* A ~~sheet~~ *STREET*
5. ___*C*___ Tabitha   *E.* Disciple of Damascus

B. SHORT ANSWER

6. Cornelius was a __*centurian*__ of the __*Italian*__ band.

7. In __*Joppa*__ Peter fell into a __*trance*__ at about the __*ninth*__ hour.

8. Peter healed __*Aeneas*__ who was sick with the __*palsey*__ for __8 years__ and raised __*Tabitha or*__ from the dead.
    (Dorcas)

C. TRUE OR FALSE

9. __*F*___ The men that went with Saul from Damascus did not hear the voice of the Lord as he spoke to Saul.

10. __*T*___ Paul pronounced judgement upon Elymas the sorcerer.

D. MEMORY VERSE

11. Quote 10:44

While Peter yet spake these words, the Holy Ghost fell on all them which heard the word.

64

Chapters 9 & 10
STUDY ACTIVITY

Vocabulary - Matching

~~C~~ 1. Pricks 9:5   A. To wait for

H 2. Confounded 9:22   B. Three times

A 3. Tarried 9:43   C. A sharp point/thorn

E 4. Centurion 10:1   D. A state resembling sleep

B 5. Thrice 10:16   E. Military officer

G 6. Gainsaying 10:29   F. Improved spiritually

D 7. Trance 10:10   G. To contradict/oppose

F 8. Edified 9:31   H. Confused/overwhelmed

True or false

False 9. The disciples took Saul early in the morning and let him down by the wall in a basket.

True 10. Saul disputed against the Grecians.

True 11. Lydda was neigh (near) Joppa.

~~True~~ False 12. The (women) *widows* were weeping and shewing the coats and garments which Dorcas made.

Characters & Locations

Saul 13. He wanted to bring men and women bound to Jerusalem.

Ananias 14. He was the one who laid hands on Saul as the scales fell from his eyes.

Barnabas 15. He told the disciples how Saul had preached boldly at Damascus in the Name of Jesus.

Peter 16. He came down to the saints at Lydda.

Aeneas 17. He was sick of the palsy and eight years in bed.

Dorcas 18. She was a woman full of good works and almsdeeds.

mon a tanner 19. Peter dwelt at his house and tarried there many days.

Cornelius 20. He was a centurion of the Italian Band.

65

Chapters 9 & 10
STUDY ACTIVITY

Characters & Locations

Lydda 21. Where Aeneas dwelt.

Joppa 22. Where Tabitha lived.

Saron 23. The people in Lydda and _____ saw Aeneas healed.

Straight 24. The street where Judas lived.

Damascus 25. City were Ananias lived.

Thought Questions

26. Describe Peter's vision.
He saw as it had been a great white sheet knit at the four corners let down to earth. On it were common or unclean beasts.

27. What did Peter's vision mean.
That no man is common or unclean.

To me.... (God created all men equal. No one is better than another. The Jew is no better than the Gentile, the black is no better than the white, the Intellectual man is no better than the unlearned man. No matter who you are or what you are, you mean something to God. You are Somebody. Everybody is Somebody. Salvation is offered to everybody. And its free.)

2

CHARACTER/LOCATION WORD SEARCH

Briefly describe the following characters and locations, then find and circle them in the word search.

Saul _Persecuter of the disciples Saints of God_
Barnabas _Told people Paul preached_
Aeneas _sick of the palsey and in bed for eight years_
Ananias _the one who layed hands on Saul, prayed for him, scales fell off_
Peter
Straight Street _where Judas lived_
Damacus _Ananias the desiple lived there_
Caesarea _where Cornelius lived_
Samaria
Lydda _where Aeneas lived and was healed_
Judaea _The word was published throughout all Judea_
Joppa _where Tabitha lived_
Saron _Said Aeneas Aeneas healed_
Galilee _Word was preached throughout_
Tabitha _made ;tems for the Widows_
Dorcas _another name for Tabitha (interperted)_
Simon the Tanner _where Peter dwelt_
Cornelius _a Centurion of the "Italian Band"_

```
S A I N A N A A J U D
I H S A N J U D A E A
M T A S G B O J U A D
O I M G T A B P S P T
N B A A H R O R P S E
T A R L O N S S I A E
H T I I T A U V G R R
E T A L H B C Z N O T
T P M E N A A D A N S
A E N E A S M D D G T
N M S G V O A L D R H
N N T R A T D U Y I G
E S E A G N D Y L S I
R E T E P T L Y A G A
A E R A S E A C T I R
S U I L E N R O C A T
D U J A T O C E R T S
M O A N D Y L S G R S
```

NAME _Sis. Delores Williams_
CLASS _Bro. Cargle #2_
DATE _1-25-81_

67

QUARTERLY REVIEW EXAMINATION -- CHAPTERS 1-10

86% / 86%

NAME _Sis. Delores Williams_ CLASS _Bro. Cargle's_

Short Answer

Name the eleven original apostles and the one elected to replace Judas Iscarot:

1. _Barthowlemew_ 2. _John_ 3. _James son of Alphe_
4. _James_ 5. _Phillip_ 6. _Mathew_
7. _Simon Zelotes_ 8. _Thomas_ 9. _Peter_
10. _Judas bro. of James_ 11. _Stephen_ 12. _Mathias_

Name the seven Deacons:

13. _Stephen_ 14. _Phillip_ 15. _P✗ Prochorus_
16. _Nicanor_ 17. _✗ Parmenas_ 18. _Thomas✗_
19. _Nicholas_   _Timon_

Name the five synagogues who disputed with Stephen:

20✗ _____ 21✗ _____ 22✗ _____

23✗ _____ 24✗ _____

Name twelve of the many groups of people who were present in Jerusalem on the day of Pentecost: _Partheians_

25. _Partheians_ 26. _Phrigia_ 27. _Strangers of Rom_
28. _Medes_ 29. _Pamphyllia_ 30. _Jews_
31. _Asia_ 32. _Mespotamia_ 33. _Proselytes_
34. _R+ Lybia_ 35. _Egypt_ 36. _Elamites_

Name the four kinds of creatures Peter saw in his vision:

37. _4 footed beasts_ 38. _Creaping things_ 39. _fowels of the air_
40. _Wild beasts_

Name eight Old Testament Characters mentioned in Acts Chapters 1-10:

41. _Moses_ 42. _Jacob_ 43. _Joseph_
44. _Abraham_ 45. _David_ 46✗
47✗ _Isiack_ 48. _Isiah_

68

Character Matching

_G_ 49. Luke   A. He was not chosen to replace Judas Iscariot

_L_ 50. Theophilus   B. Died within three hours of Ananias

_A_ 51. Joseph Barsabas Justus   C. He baptized the Eunuch

_N_ 52. Caiaphas   D. Queen of the Ethiopians

_D_ 53. Candace   E. Sold a possession and kept back a part

_M_ 54. Ethiopian Eunuch   F. He boasted to be somebody

_O_ 55. Stephen   G. He is said to have written Acts

_C_ 56. Philip   H. Asked alms at the Temple

_K_ 57. Saul   I. Doctor of law and a Pharisee

_J_ 58. Dorcas/Tabitha   J. Was raised from the dead

_E_ 59. Ananias   K. He made havock in the church

_B_ 60. Sapphira   L. The Acts were written to him

_H_ 61. The Lame Man   M. He was reading the prophet Esaias

_I_ 62. Gamaliel   N. A high priest

_F_ 63. Theudas   O. The first martyr

True & False

True 64. Mount Olivet was a Sabbath day's journey from Jerusalem.

False 65. There were about 150 (120) people in the upper room.

True 66. Aceldama means field of blood.

True 67. The Prophet Isaiah told that in the last days God would pour out his spirit.

True 68. The hour of prayer is the ninth hour.

True 69. The Temple was called the Temple Beautiful.

True 70. The lame man was above 40 years old.

False 71. John told the lame man that he had no gold or silver.

True/False 72. God appeared to Abraham in Mesopotamia.

False 73. Simeon (Simon) offered money for the power to lay hands for the giving of the Holy Ghost.

True 74. Jacob begat twelve patriarchs.

True 75. Simon was a Sorcerer.

True 76. The Angel of the Lord told Philip to go unto Gaza.

True 77. After the Spirit caught Philip away he was found at Azotus.

False 78. As he was traveling away from Damascus, Saul heard a voice saying, "Saul, Saul why persecutest thou me?"

True 79. Saul was three days without sight.

True 80. The house of Ananias was on the street called Straight.

True 81. Aeneas was sick of palsy for eight years.

True 82. Tabitha dwelt at Joppa.

False 83. At Joppa Philip stayed with Simon a tanner. *Simon Peter*

False 84. Cornelius was a centurion and a devout man.

False 85. Peter was surnamed Simon.

True 86. About the sixth hour Peter fell into a trance and saw a vision.

False 87. Cornelius sent two (3) men to Joppa.

False 88. In Peter's vision the same thing happened thrice.

Multiple Choice

D 89. Jesus was seen after his passion for a) 10 days b) 20 days c) 30 days (d) 40 days

B 90. Pentecost is associated with the number a) 5 (b) 50 c) 500 d) 5000

A 91. While the disciples looked toward heaven, there appeared in white apparel (a) 2 men b) 3 men c) 4 men d) 5 men

D 92. The council marvelled at Peter and John because they were perceived to be a) unlearned b) ignorant c) both a & b (d) neither a nor b

D 93. Joses was surnamed a) Philip b) John c) Ananias (d) Barnabas

D 94. The apostles were imprisoned by a) Thedus b) Joses c) both a & b (d) neither a nor b

A 95. Satan filled his heart and made him lie to the Holy Ghost (a) Ananias b) Sapphira c) both a & b d) neither a nor b

C 96. In chapters 1 - 10, how many different men named Judas are mentioned a) 2 b) 3 (c) 4 d) 5

A 97. The Grecians, because of their widows, murmured against the (a) Hebrews b) Pharisees c) Chaldaens (d) none of the above

D 98. Isaac was circumcised on the a) 5th day b) 6th day c) 7th day (d) 8th day

C 99. Because of persecution many were scattered to a) Judaea b) Samaria (c) both a & b d) neither a nor b

D 100. During his journeys, Philip traveled to a) Gaza b) Azotus c) Caesarea (d) all of the above.

70

Sis. Delores Williams *90%*

Bro. Cargle

TEST #6   CHAPTERS 11 & 12

A. MEMORY VERSE ACTS 11:16

1. Then remembered I the words of the _Lord_, how that he said, _John_ indeed _baptized_ with _water_ ; but ye shall be _baptized_ with the _Holy_ _Ghost_ .

B. TRUE OR FALSE

2. _True_ The Apostles contended with Peter about eating with the Gentiles.

3. _False_ Peter went to Caesarea to meet with three men Cornelius had sent.

4. _False_ While Herod was governor he killed James and John with the Sword.

5. _True_ Peter was arrested with the intent of bringing him forth to the people after Easter.

6. _False_ Disciples were first called Christians at Antioch.

C. SHORT ANSWER

7. Who answered Peter's knock at the door? _desiples_

8. What was John's surname? _Mark_ .

9. What was Simon's surname? _Peter_ .

D. MATCH

10. _B_ Agabus   a. Mark

     _A_ John   b. Prophet

     _E_ Simon   c. Chamberlain

     _C_ Blastus   d. Damsel

     _D_ Rhoda   e. Peter

71

Study Activity
Chapters 11 & 12

Name _Sis Delores Williams_ Class _Bro. Cargles Class_

True & False

1. _True_ The vision Peter saw contained fourfooted beasts of
the earth and wild beasts, and creeping things and fowls of the
air.
2. _False_ Two men sent from caesarea came to the house where
Peter was.
3. _True_ Simon's surname is Peter.
4. _True_ John baptized with water.
5. _True_ X In Phenice, and Cyprus, and Antioch, Stephen traveled
preaching the word to the Jews only.
6. _True_ The disciples were called Christians first in Antioch.
7. _False_ Herod the governor, vexed the chruch. _Certain of the church_
8. _False_ When Rhoda heard Peter's voice, she opend the gate for
gladness.
9. _True_ Blastus was made the king's chamberlain.
10. _True_ Herod was eaten of worms.

Character Matching

_H G_ 11. John   A. Damsel
_H_ 12. Rhoda   B. Peter
_F_ 13. Herod   C. Mark
_B_ 14. Simon   D. Caesar
_E_ 15. Agabus   E. Signified a great dearth
_D_ 16. Claudius   F. Smote by an Angel
_I_ 17. Barnabas   G. Instructed to arise and eat
_G H_ 18. Peter   H. Baptized with water
_J_ 19. James   I. Sent to the elders
_C_ 20. John   J. Killed with a sword

Vocabulary- Multiple choice

21. Expounded 11:4   a) preached   (b) explained   c) hit
22. Tidings 11:22   (a) news   b) ocean   c) people
23. Cleave 11:23   a) witness   b) pray   (c) stay close
24. Signified 11:28   a) angered   (b) told   c) knew
25. Gird 12:8   a) to get dressed b) to kneel   (c) to encircle
                                                                  clothing with a
                                                                  band or cord
26. Damsel 12:13   a) young woman   b) young man   (x) child
27. Abode 12:19   a) wandering   (b) stayed   c) left
28. Arrayed 12:21   (a) dressed impressively b) crowned c) healthy

72

29. Chamberlain 12:20   (a) officer in the king's household
                         b) relative   c) an advisor

30. Oration 12:21   a) confession   b) Celebration   (c) speech

Thought Questions

31. How was Peter released from prison
An Angel of the Lord came in a light, told him to get dressed and follow him. He led him past the first and second ward, through the iron gate which opened unto them, and through one street. Then disappeared.

32. How did the disciples react to the escape and return of Peter?
When Rhoda told them he was at the gate first they thought she was mad, then they said it was his angel. He kept knocking so they opened the door and were astonished.

33. How did Herod react to Peter's escape?
He examined the keepers and commanded that they should be put to death. He went and abode in Caesarea.

34. What was Herod's end? Why?
He was slain by an Angel of the Lord, and eaten of worms because when he gave his oration he gave not the Glory to God.

35. How did Peter defend preaching to the Gentiles?
He told the apostles and bretheren (in detail) about his dream and what God said ("What God hath cleansed, that call not thou common) and about the three men coming from Caesarea for him, and what the man told him (Cornelius) He told them that the Holy Ghost fell on them like it did to the others in the beginning

73

WORD SEARCH

Make a list of the ten characters and the nine places named in Acts Chapter 11. Find and circle the characters and places you find, in order to determine what character and what place has been left out.

Character _Stephen_   Place _Cyrene_

J	E	S	U	S	C	H	R	I	S	T	J
E	C	Y	P	R	U	S	J	D	D	J	O
R	I	C	H	I	S	N	S	O	R	E	H
U	N	P	P	S	U	B	A	G	A	S	N
S	E	C	H	I	A	E	U	L	S	J	T
T	H	S	C	M	R	E	L	A	E	U	H
O	P	D	O	O	A	E	J	U	A	D	E
P	O	H	I	N	E	I	E	P	C	A	B
P	J	I	T	N	T	A	R	S	S	E	A
A	L	E	N	N	I	G	R	A	U	A	P
S	A	B	A	N	R	A	B	S	I	D	T
A	L	J	P	I	L	N	E	U	D	C	I
L	E	H	P	E	T	E	R	S	U	L	S
E	M	N	O	I	G	I	T	R	A	A	T
M	T	T	J	E	R	U	S	A	L	E	M
C	A	E	S	A	R	Z	E	A	T	C	U	E

10 characters
1. Peter
2. Simon
3. Stephen
4. Barnabas
5. Saul
6. Agabus
7. Claudius Caesar
8. Jesus Christ
9.
10.

9 Places
1. Judaea
2. Jerusalem
3. Joppa
4. Caesarea
5. Antioch
6. Phenice
7. Cyprus
8. Cyrene
9. Tarsus

NAME_____   CLASS_____

disciples
Christians
elders
apostles
brethren

74

WORD SEARCH

Make a list of the eleven characters and five places named in ^Acts Chapter 12. Find and circle the characters and places you find, in order to determine what character and what place has been left out.

Character _____ *Peter* _____ Place _____ *Type* _____

B	A	R	N	A	B	A	S	B	L	A	S	T	D
J	E	R	U	S	A	L	A	T	I	N	T	R	R
H	E	R	R	O	N	C	U	R	M	A	O	B	N
C	E	A	R	O	O	L	L	E	M	L	E	L	N
A	D	R	E	E	D	S	L	A	E	R	S	A	E
E	N	O	O	W	I	A	W	H	E	E	D	S	N
S	M	N	A	D	S	A	T	N	M	D	W	T	H
A	I	F	E	U	T	F	M	A	U	R	H	U	O
R	H	O	R	H	O	H	J	R	A	D	O	S	J
E	J	E	O	L	H	N	E	A	H	M	E	S	T
A	J	K	E	I	N	J	G	K	O	O	F	Y	A
N	T	G	J	U	D	A	E	A	I	O	D	R	C
H	N	A	Z	X	B	Y	C	D	A	N	E	A	J
A	K	R	K	R	A	M	N	H	O	J	G	M	K

11
Characters
1. John
2. Rhoda
3. Herod
4. James
5. Peter
6. Mary
7. Blastus
8. Barnabus
9. Saul
10. Mark
11. Angel

5
Places
1. Caesarea
2. Tyre
3. Sidon
4. Jerusalem
5. Judaea

Name_____ Class_____

God
angel,
Lord

75

Sis. Delores Williams.
Bro. Cargle's Class
78 0/0

TEST #7   ACTS CHAPTERS 13 & 14

A.   MATCHING

1.   _D_   Herod   A.   Minister
2.   _A_   John   B.   Elymas
3.   _B_   Barjesus   C.   Benjamite
4.   _E_   Sergius Paulus   D.   Tetrarch
5.   _C_   Cis   E.   Deputy

B.   TRUE OR FALSE

6.   _True_   In Lystra the people called Paul, Jupiter and Barnabas they called Mercurius.

7.   _True_   Certain Jews from Antioch and Iconium stoned Paul.

8.   _True_   Barnabas, Simeon, Lucius and Manaen were in the church at Antioch.

C.   SHORT ANSWER

9.   Name the 10 places visited during the First Missionary Journey _Antioch am Pamph_ _131?_
Lystra, _Cyprus_, _Iconium_, _Sergius of Permagie_ _Cyrene_,
Salamis, _Isle of Pamphos_ _Antioch_,

D.   MEMORY VERSE

10.   Nevertheless he _left_ not _us_ without a _Witness_ in that he did _____, and gave us _fruit_ from _____, and _____ _____ _____ our _____ with _____ and _____.

Sunday-Quarter Exam
Chapts. 1-14

Sis. Delores Williams
Bro. Carple's Class

STUDY ACTIVITY
Chapters 13 & 14

Vocabulary - Matching

___E___ 1. Tetrarch   A. Decay

___O___ 2. Thence   B. Mocking abuse of God

___I___ 3. Testimony   C. Filled with jealous ill will

___A___ 4. Corruption   D. A wreath of flowers

___J___ 5. Perish   E. Ruler of a fourth part

___N___ 6. Congregation   F. Tore

___C___ 7. Envy   G. Offering

___B___ 8. Blaspheming   H. Increased in strength

___M___ 9. Waxed   I. Affirmation

___K___ 10. Lo   J. Go from sight

___L___ 11. Eternal   K. Look/see

___D___ 12. Garlands   L. Without end

___G___ 13. Sacrifice   M. Oppression

___F___ 14. Rent   N. Religious gathering of people

___H___ 15. Tribulation   O. That place

Chronological Order
Put the following cities (from chapter 13) in the order they were
visited during the missionary journeys: SELEUCIA, SALAMIS, ICONIUM,
ANTIOCH, ANTIOCH IN PISIDIA, CYPRUS, PAPHOS, PERGIA IN PAMPHYLIA

① Antioch

16. *② Seleucia*   17. *③ Cyprus*

18. *④ Salamis*   19. *⑤ Paphos*

20. *⑥ Pergia in Pamphylia*   21. *⑦ Antioch in Pisidia*

22. *⑧ Iconium*   23. _____

Multiple Choice

24. Barnabas was called (a) Jupiter   b) Mercurius   c) Paul   d) both a&b

25. Barjesus was   a) Elymas   (b) A false prophet   c) a Jew   d) all of the above

26. Sergius was   a) Governor   (b) deputy   c) Paulus   d) a&b   e) b&c

77

Study Activity
Chapters 13 & 14
Page 2

27. Saul was a a) King (b) Son of Cis   c) Of the tribe of Benjamin d) All of the above.

28. Simeon was called a) Cyrene (b) Niger   c) Paulus d) Peter

29. Lucius was of a) Antioch b) Paphos c) Iconium (d) Cyrene

30. Manaen was brought up with (a) Herod b) Simeon c) Lucius d) All of the above

True & False

True 31. Saul is also called Paul in this lesson.

True 32. Saul told Barjesus he would be blind for a season.

True 33. Sergius Paulus was a prudent man.

True 34. Israel had judges for about the space of 450 years.

False 35. Saul was the son of Benjamin.

True 36. David was the son of Jesse.

False 37. The old testament scripture mentioned in Acts 13 is second Psalms.

False 38. The impotent man from Lystra had been cripple for eight years.

True 39. The people of Lystra called Paul and Barnabas gods.

True 40. Paul was stoned.

Chronological Order
        Put the following cities(from chapter 14) in the order they were
        visited during the missionary journeys. They started from Iconium:
        ANTIOCH (USE TWICE),ATTALIA, DERBE, LYSTRA (USE TWICE), ICONIUM,
        PAMPHYLIA, PERGA, PISIDIA.

41. _____   42. _____

43. _____   44. _____

45. _____   46. _____

47. _____   48. _____

49. _____   50. _____

NAME _____   CLASS _____

78

VOCABULARY WORDSEARCH
13 & 14

```
A U T S D N A L R A G S B V
C C C H D W X D E T R A L C
Y O O T E E T H E N C E E A
T N H R F N Z C U X G R C R
H G G I P L C R T J A L U U
C R N B K U L A E M N W F P
S E E U R Q P R S P O P I I
W G A L A N E T N E R R T
T A X A Y V N E L V R I C O
L T D T E A I T M O N C A E
A I N I A G S T O Y N E S A
M O D O X A A V N N N I B G
H N T N D W H R Y E R O L I
E T E R N A L A L E O O T H
F D G N I M E H P S A L B C
```

Find and circle the meanings of the following words:

decay _Corruption_   Go from sight _perish_

Mocking abuse of God _Blaspheming_ Look/see _Lo_

Filled with jealous ill will _Envy_   Without end _Eternal_

A wreath of flowers _Garlands_   Oppression _Waxed_

Ruler over a fourth part _Tetrarch_ Tore _Rent_

Religious gathering of people _Congregation_

Offering _Sacrifice_   That place _Thence_

Increased in strength _~~Testimony~~ Waxed_ Affirmation _Testimony_

Tribulation ~~Tribulation~~

79

WORD CROSS
13 & 14

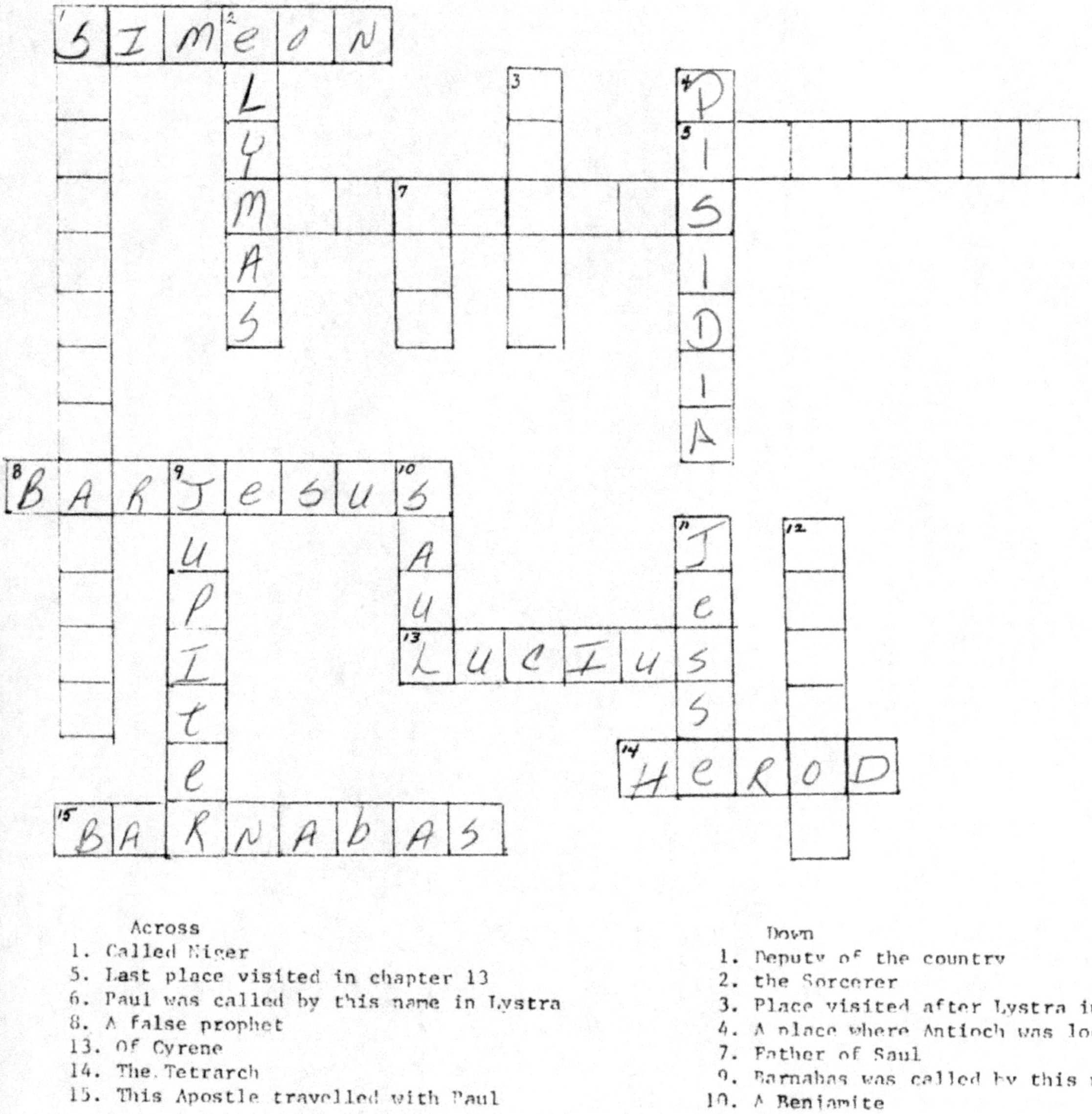
SIMEON
LYMAS
PISIDIA
BARJESUS
JUPITER
SAUL
LUCIUS
JESSE
HEROD
BARNABAS

Across
1. Called Niger
5. Last place visited in chapter 13
6. Paul was called by this name in Lystra
8. A false prophet
13. Of Cyrene
14. The Tetrarch
15. This Apostle travelled with Paul

Down
1. Deputy of the country
2. the Sorcerer
3. Place visited after Lystra in Chap.
4. A place where Antioch was located
7. Father of Saul
9. Barnabas was called by this name
10. A Benjamite
11. Father of David
12. The fifth place visited in Chap. 13

Memory Verse 15:9

Study Activity
Chapters 15 & 16

Name *Sis Delores Williams*   Class *Bro. Cargle's*

Vocabulary Matching

I 1. Disputation   A. Making Clean
F 2. Conversion   B. The Remnant
A 3. Purifying   C. Unsettling one in his faith
O 4. Tempt   D. Comfort
J 5. Yoke   E. The district of a town
B 6. Residue   F. Adoption of Christianity
L 7. Abstain   G. Accustomed
C 8. Subverting   H. Fortune telling
K 9. Epistle   I. Provoking debate
D 10. Consolation   J. Bondage/ oppresive servitude
E 11. Quarters   K. A letter
N 12. Elders   L. Have nothing to do with
G 13. Wont   M. Roman army commanders or rulers
H 14. Soothsaying   N. One having authority by virtue of age or experience
M 15. Magistrates   O. Put to the test

Very good.

True & False

True 16. A certain sect of Pharisees wanted to command the gentiles to keep the law of moses

True 17. The gentiles were commanded to abstain from meats offered to idols.

True 18. Judas and Silas were prophets.

False 19. Mark's surname was John.

True 20. There was sharp contention between Barnabas and Paul as they departed asunder one from the other.

True 21. Paul and Silas were forbidden of the Holy Ghost to preach the word in Asia.

False 22. A man of Macedonia visited Paul at night and asked him to come over to Macedonia and help.

False 23. Macedonia is the chief city of Philippi.

False 24. And at the ninth hour Paul and Silas prayed and an earthquake caused the prison doors to be opened.

True 25. Lydia, a seller of purple, was of the city of Thatira.

81

WORD SEARCH

List all locations mentioned in chapters 13 & 16 and then circle them in the word search.(if a name is mentioned more than once use it only one time)

1. Judaea   2. Phenice   3. Samaria
4. Jerusalem   5. Antioch   6. Syria
7. Cilicia   8. Cyprus   9. Derbe
10. Lystra   11. Phrygia   12. Galatia
13. Mysia   14. Bithynia   15. Troas
16. Samothreia   17. Neapolis   18. Philippi
19. Thyatira   20. Pamphylia   21. Iconium
22. Asia   23. Macedonia

```
T  M  U  I  N  O  C  I  A  U  O  P  I  G
Y  Y  C  T  E  H  P  A  I  C  J  H  E  I
H  S  Y  R  O  P  I  O  T  O  U  P  R  R
P  I  O  J  I  T  S  Y  R  I  A  Y  E  E
M  A  T  L  A  M  N  E  O  T  D  G  M  N
A  H  U  L  I  A  O  C  C  H  E  I  K  T
H  H  A  F  L  C  A  I  R  I  A  M  A  S  I
P  G  A  C  Y  E  I  H  H  J  E  I  A  A
H  H  B  H  H  D  C  E  P  U  L  U  M  I
E  A  I  I  P  O  I  H  E  D  A  Y  O  N
N  R  C  L  M  N  L  P  M  A  S  U  T  O
T  T  H  Y  A  T  I  P  A  E  U  T  H  D
T  S  U  R  P  Y  C  T  B  A  R  J  R  E
A  Y  D  J  L  S  A  R  T  P  E  B  A  C
L  L  E  X  M  R  E  O  T  H  J  T  C  A
L  L  Y  S  T  D  P  A  S  U  R  I  I  M
N  E  A  P  O  L  I  S  P  Y  I  M  A  A
```

NAME _____   class _____

Sis. Delores Williams
Bro. Cargle's Class

TEST #8   CHAPTERS 15 & 16

A. SHORT ANSWER

1. What question did Paul and Barnabas take to the Council at Jerusalem?
    did the Gentiles have to keep the law of Moses, be circumcised in order to be saved.

2. What was the Law of Moses the Pharisees wanted the Gentiles to keep?
    circumcision.

3. Who made the final decision at the Council in Jerusalem? *Peter*.

4. Name the person who caused the contention between Paul and Barnabas
    John Mark.

B. TRUE OR FALSE

5. *True* Barnabas chose Silas and went to Syria.
6. *True* Timotheus' mother was Jewess and his father was a Greek.
7. *True* The Holy Ghost stopped Paul from Preaching the word in Asia.
8. *False* Lydia was of the city of Neapolis and she was a seller of purple

C. MEMORY VERSE   ACTS 15:29

9. That ye *abstain* from *Meats* *offered* to *idols*,
    and from *blood*, and from *things* *strangled*, and from
    fornication : from which if ye *keep* *yourselves*
    ye shall do *well*. Fare *ye* *well*.

D. 10. Explain why Paul was jailed and how he was freed.
    ① the soothsayers, of the possessed damsel was angry that she had been delivered. They lied to the magistrates. The magistrates commanded the jailer to keep them safely.
    ② At midnight Paul and Silas prayed and sang praises to God. the Lord sent an earthquake and shook the prison and everyone bands and stocks fell off.

83

STUDY ACTIVITY
CHAPTERS 17 & 18

Name _Sis. Delores Williams_ Class _Bro. Cargle's_ *E*

Vocabulary – Matching

H 1. Raiment   A. Rising Against

A 2. Insurrection   B. Spoke/persuaded

L 3. Lewdness   C. Solemn promise

F 4. Shorn   D. Fluent, very expressive

C 5. Vow   E. Attacked

O 6. Bade   F. Cut in order to remove

M 7. Saluted   G. Idle/low class

D 8. Eloquent   H. Dress/clothes

I 9. Fervent   I. Zealous, eager, earnest

N 10. Consorted *B*   J. One who looks for the principles that regulate the universe

G 11. Baser   K. Full of

B *O* 12. Reasoned   L. Lasciviousness

E 13. Assaulted   M. To honor in a formal manner

K 14. Wholly   N. Cast lots with

J 15. Philosophers   O. Told

Multiple Choice

D 16. Paul passed through a) Amphipolis   b) Apollonica   c) Thessalonica d) a & b

A 17. Paul waited for Silas and Timotheus at a) Athens   b) Troas c) Ephesus   d) none of the above

D 18. Aquila was a) Priscilla's husband   b) born in Pontus   c) a tent maker d) all of the above

B 19. Apollos was a) a gentile   b) a Jew   c) born at Corinth   d) born at Ephesus

A *C* 20. This man was chief ruler of the synagogue   a) Crispus   b) Sosthenes c) both a & b   d) neither a nor b

84

True and False

True 21. Claudius commanded all Jews to depart from Rome.

True 22. Paul's occupation was tentmaker.

True 23. Paul stayed a year and six months at Corinth.

False = True 24. The Epicureans and Stoicks stood with Paul against the Greeks.

True 25. Paul spoke to the men of Athens at Mars Hill.

True 26. Paul reasoned in the synagogue every sabbath.

False 27. Silas and Timotheus left Paul and went to Macedonia.

True 28. Priscilla and Aquila sailed to Syria with Paul.

False 29. Dionysius wanted to stone Paul.

False 30. A man named Damaris clave unto Paul.

17 & 18

WORD   SCRAMBLE

Unscramble the following locations and place them in chronological
order   according to when Paul passed through or stayed there.

```
I O H R C T              S I R Y              E A T S N H
A H E R E C C N          A E R B              E S S H U P
I Q E A C L N S H S T    R E S A C A E A      L A A I O O C N P I
I T N A H C O            A I I O S L P H P M  A T A G A L I
R I H G A P
```

1. _Amphipolis_   2. _Apollonia_
3. _Thessalonica_   4. _Berea_ (5) _Athens_
(6) _Corinth_   (7) _Syria_ (8) _Cenchrea_
(9) _Ephesus_   (10) _Caesarea_
(11) _Antioch_   (12) _Galatia_
(13) _Phrygia_   12. _____

13. _____

Name_____   Class _____

86

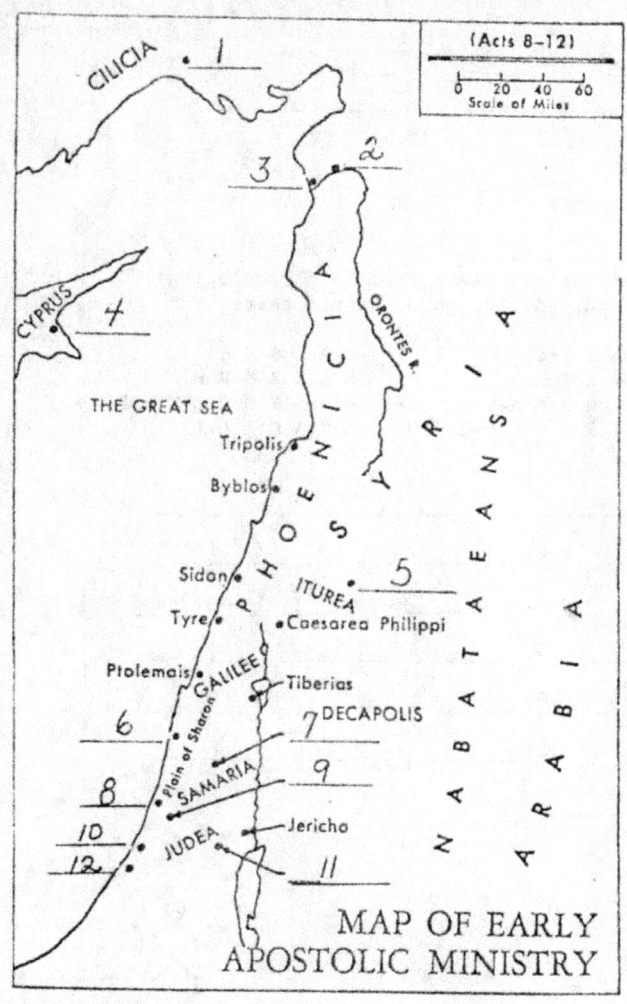

(Acts 8-12)

Scale of Miles 0 20 40 60

MAP OF EARLY APOSTOLIC MINISTRY

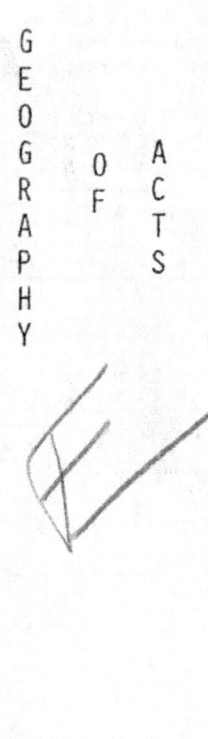

GEOGRAPHY OF ACTS

Name the places that match the numbers on the above map, then write the name of the place on the line below that has the same number.

The places you are to find are: ANTIOCH, AZOTUS, CAESAREA, DAMASCUS, GAZA, JERUSALEM, JOPPA, LYDDA, SALAMIS, SAMARIA, SELEUCIA, TARSUS.

1. Tarsus
2. Antioch
3. Seleucia
4. Salamis
5. Damascus
6. Caesarea
7. Samaria
8. Joppa
9. Lydda
10. Azotus
11. Jerusalem
12. Gaza

Name _____   Class _____

87

GEOGRAPHY OF ACTS

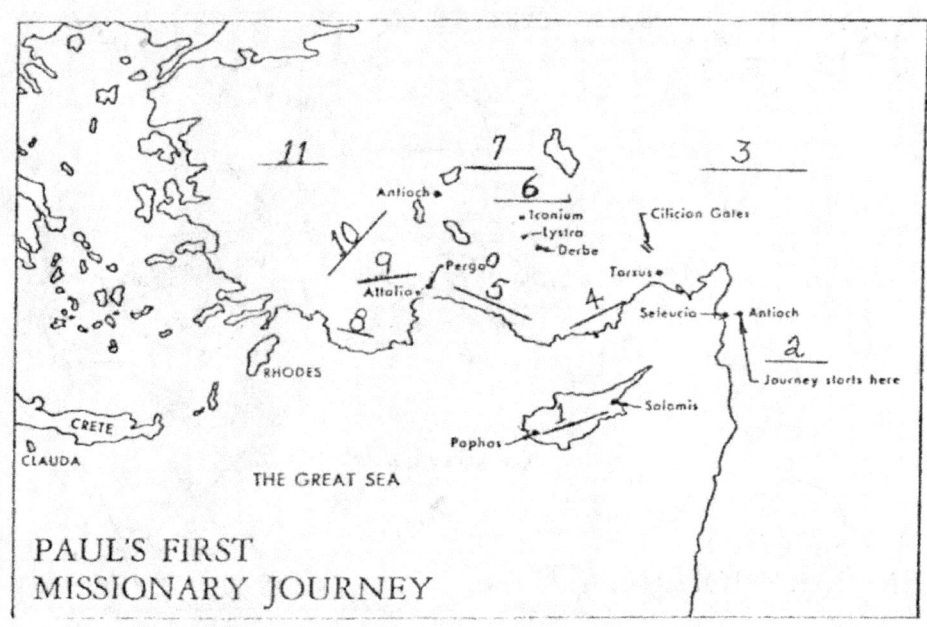

PAUL'S FIRST
MISSIONARY JOURNEY

Name the places that match the numbers on the above map, then write the
name of the place on the line below that has the same number.

The places you are to find are: ASIA, CAPPADOCIA, CILICIA, CYPRUS, GALATIA,
LYCAONIA, LYSIA, PAMPHYLIA, PHRYGIA, PISIDIA, SYRIA.

1. Cyprus
2. Syria
3. Cappadocia
4. Cilicia
5. Pamphylia
6. Lycaonia
7. Galatia
8. Lysia
9. Pisidia
10. Phrygia
11. Asia

Draw a line and connect all of the places Paul visited on his first
missionary journey. (Draw on the map and use a colored pencil if possible)

Name_____   Class_____

88